JACOB TREMBLAY

BY MARY BLECKWEHL

AMICUS LEARNING

Inspire is published by
Amicus Learning, an imprint of Amicus
P.O. Box 227
Mankato, MN 56002
www.amicuspublishing.us

Editor: Ana Brauer
Series Designer: Kathleen Petelinsek
Book Designer and Photo Researcher: Emily Dietz

Library of Congress Cataloging-in-Publication Data
Names: Bleckwehl, Mary E. author
Title: Jacob Tremblay / Mary Bleckwehl.
Description: Mankato : Amicus Learning, 2026. | Series: Inspire | Includes bibliographical references and index. | Audience: Ages 5–9 | Audience: Grades 2–3 | Summary: "Lights, camera, action! Discover how Jacob Tremblay became a young Hollywood star in the movies *Room*, *Wonder*, and *Luca*. This engaging biography includes a table of contents, glossary, further resources, and index" —Provided by publisher.
Identifiers: LCCN 2025011928 (print) | LCCN 2025011929 (ebook) | ISBN 9798892008617 library binding | ISBN 9798892009270 paperback | ISBN 9798892009935 ebook
Subjects: LCSH: Tremblay, Jacob—Juvenile fiction | Motion picture actors and actresses—Canada—Biography—Juvenile literature | LCGFT: Biographies
Classification: LCC PN2308.T74 B74 2025 (print) | LCC PN2308.T74 (ebook) | DDC 791.4302/8092—dc23/eng/20250417
LC record available at https://lccn.loc.gov/2025011928
LC ebook record available at https://lccn.loc.gov/2025011929

Photo Credits: Alamy Stock Photo/Album, 17, Cinematic Collection, 6, Kathy Hutchins, 16, TCD/Prod.DB, 10, 14; Associated Press/Alex J. Berliner, 21, Sthanlee B. Mirador, cover; Getty Images/ Gotham, 5, Gregg DeGuire, 13, Steve Granitz, 9; Newscom/Brett D. Cove / SplashNews, 18; Shutterstock/Dan Jamieson, 8

Printed in the United States of America

Table of Contents

Rising Star

Jacob Tremblay is a Canadian television and movie actor. He has played many different roles. He became famous after starring in *Room* (2015). Tremblay has also voiced animated characters. This young actor is full of talent!

Jacob Tremblay started acting at a young age and quickly became well known.

Tremblay's first movie role was in *The Smurfs 2* (2013).

A Very Young Actor

Tremblay was acting before he knew what it was. He was in toy commercials as a toddler. It felt like playing to him. He landed his first big role at five years old. He starred as Blue in *The Smurfs 2* (2013).

Early Breakout Role

It didn't take long for Tremblay to get noticed. At age eight, he was cast in the movie *Room* (2015). He played a boy who lived in a shed with his **kidnapped** mom. His role earned him many awards.

THE FORCE IS WITH HIM

Tremblay is a *Star Wars* fan. He keeps his acting awards next to his Millennium Falcon starship.

Tremblay won a Critics' Choice award for his work in *Room* (2015).

Tremblay played Auggie, a boy who teaches others about kindness, in *Wonder* (2017).

Boy Wonder

Actors sometimes have to change their looks for a role. Tremblay starred in the movie *Wonder* (2017). His character was a boy with facial differences. For the role, he wore face **prosthetics**, a wig, and fake teeth.

A Family of Actors

Tremblay's inspiration for acting came from his own love of play. His family influenced him, too. His father was a child actor. Tremblay's sisters, Emma and Erica, are also actors.

DID YOU KNOW?

Tremblay and his sisters acted together in a short film called *Santa's Little Ferrets* (2016).

Tremblay with his parents and sisters, Erica (left) and Emma (center), at an event for *Wonder*.

Tremblay has acted in movies for older viewers, including *Good Boys* (2019) and *Room*.

Up for a Challenge

This actor doesn't like being bored. He loves playing different characters. Landing a part isn't easy. But Tremblay has done it many times. Acting is fun for him. He can pretend to be someone else.

DID YOU KNOW?
More than 2,000 kids tried out for *Room*. Tremblay landed the role.

Voice Actor

Tremblay is also a **voice actor**. The guitar-playing Pete the Cat can talk and sing. It's Tremblay's voice in the TV series. Two of his voice roles were sea creatures. In *Luca* (2021), he voiced the lead role. He was Flounder's voice in *The Little Mermaid* live-action movie (2023).

HIS VOICE GETS NOTICED!
In 2025, Tremblay won a Children's & Family Emmy Award for his voice role in *Orion and the Dark* (2024).

Tremblay voices Luca, a young sea monster curious about life above the water.

Tremblay encourages others to stand up for what's right.

Choosing Kindness

Tremblay started acting for fun. He found he's good at it. But he's learned much more. He feels kindness matters. His acting roles teach about differences. He's traveled and learned to respect different **cultures**. He smiles and **compliments** people. The actor hopes others will, too.

The Next Big Thing

Jacob Tremblay is a hit as an actor. He has no plans to stop. But he has a new dream. He'd like to write and direct movies. Fans may soon see him on both sides of the camera.

Tremblay attended the world premiere of Disney's ***The Little Mermaid*** in 2023.

SUPER STATS

JACOB TREMBLAY

Birthday: October 5, 2006

Birthplace: Vancouver, British Columbia

Major TV Roles: *Pete the Cat* (voice, 2017–2022); *Harley Quinn* (voice, 2019–2025)

Major Film Roles: *Room* (2015), *Wonder* (2017), *Luca* (voice, 2021), *The Little Mermaid* (voice, 2023), *The Life of Chuck* (2025)

MAJOR AWARDS

Critics' Choice Movie Award for Best Young Performer: 2016

Best Actor in Canadian Film: 2015

Children's & Family Emmy Award: 2025

GLOSSARY

kidnap To take by force and hold against a person's will in order to get money or some other valuable thing.

Millenium Falcon A make-believe starship in the Star Wars movies.

prosthetic An artificial body part.

voice actor A person who provides the voice for animated film characters.

culture The customs of a group of people.

compliment Nice things said about someone or something.

READ MORE

Kane, Bo. **Acting Monologue and Scenes for Kids!** Burbank, CA: Burbank Publishing, 2023.

Obeng, Tiffany. **Andrew Learns About Actors.** Houston, TX: Sugar Cookie Books, 2020.

Waxman, Laura Hamilton. **Cool Kid Actors.** Minneapolis, MN: Lerner Publications, 2020.

ON THE WEB

Kiddle: Jacob Tremblay
https://kids.kiddle.co/Jacob_Tremblay

The Canadian Encyclopedia
https://www.thecanadianencyclopedia.ca/en/article/jacob-tremblay

Every effort has been made to ensure that these websites are appropriate for children. However, because of the nature of the Internet, it is impossible to guarantee that these sites will remain active indefinitely or that their contents will not be altered.

INDEX

About the Author

Mary Bleckwehl is a children's author who loves cookie dough and talking to kids. She is happiest when she is biking and exploring new places. Mary lives in Minnesota with her husband and monster dog. Check out her books at marybleckwehl.com.